Winners are Planners!

This journal belongs to

••••••••••••••••••

MONDAY

6 am	
7	
8	
9	
10	
11	
12 pm	
1	
2	
3	
4	
5	
6	
7	
8	

TODAY'S GOALS:

TODAY'S REFLECTIONS:

TODAY'S AFFIRMATIONS:

Notes

TUESDAY

6 am	
7	
8	
9	
10	
11	
12 pm	
1	
2	
3	
4	
5	
6	
7	
8	

TODAY'S AFFIRMATIONS:

TODAY'S GOALS:

TODAY'S REFLECTIONS:

Notes

WEDNESDAY

6 am	
7	
8	
9	
10	
11	
12 pm	
1	
2	
3	
4	
5	
6	
7	
8	

TODAY'S GOALS:

TODAY'S REFLECTIONS:

TODAY'S AFFIRMATIONS:

Notes

THURSDAY

6 am	
7	
8	
9	
10	
11	
12 pm	
1	
2	
3	
4	
5	
6	
7	
8	

TODAY'S GOALS:

TODAY'S REFLECTIONS:

TODAY'S AFFIRMATIONS:

Notes

FRIDAY

6 am	
7	
8	
9	
10	
11	
12 pm	
1	
2	
3	
4	
5	
6	
7	
8	

TODAY'S GOALS:

TODAY'S REFLECTIONS:

TODAY'S AFFIRMATIONS:

Notes

SATURDAY

6 am	
7	
8	
9	
10	
11	
12 pm	
1	
2	
3	
4	
5	
6	
7	
8	

TODAY'S GOALS:

TODAY'S REFLECTIONS:

TODAY'S AFFIRMATIONS:

Notes

SUNDAY

6 am	
7	
8	
9	
10	
11	
12 pm	
1	
2	
3	
4	
5	
6	
7	
8	

TODAY'S GOALS:

TODAY'S REFLECTIONS:

TODAY'S AFFIRMATIONS:

Notes

MONDAY

6 am	
7	
8	
9	
10	
11	
12 pm	
1	
2	
3	
4	
5	
6	
7	
8	

TODAY'S AFFIRMATIONS:

TODAY'S GOALS:

TODAY'S REFLECTIONS:

Notes

TUESDAY

6 am	
7	
8	
9	
10	
11	
12 pm	
1	
2	
3	
4	
5	
6	
7	
8	

TODAY'S GOALS:

TODAY'S REFLECTIONS:

TODAY'S AFFIRMATIONS:

Notes

WEDNESDAY

6 am	
7	
8	
9	
10	
11	
12 pm	
1	
2	
3	
4	
5	
6	
7	
8	

TODAY'S GOALS:

TODAY'S REFLECTIONS:

TODAY'S AFFIRMATIONS:

Notes

THURSDAY

6 am	
7	
8	
9	
10	
11	
12 pm	
1	
2	
3	
4	
5	
6	
7	
8	

TODAY'S GOALS:

TODAY'S REFLECTIONS:

TODAY'S AFFIRMATIONS:

Notes

FRIDAY

6 am	
7	
8	
9	
10	
11	
12 pm	
1	
2	
3	
4	
5	
6	
7	
8	

TODAY'S GOALS:

TODAY'S REFLECTIONS:

TODAY'S AFFIRMATIONS:

Notes

SATURDAY

6 am	
7	
8	
9	
10	
11	
12 pm	
1	
2	
3	
4	
5	
6	
7	
8	

TODAY'S GOALS:

TODAY'S REFLECTIONS:

TODAY'S AFFIRMATIONS:

Notes

SUNDAY

6 am	
7	
8	
9	
10	
11	
12 pm	
1	
2	
3	
4	
5	
6	
7	
8	

TODAY'S GOALS:

TODAY'S REFLECTIONS:

TODAY'S AFFIRMATIONS:

Notes

MONDAY

6 am	
7	
8	
9	
10	
11	
12 pm	
1	
2	
3	
4	
5	
6	
7	
8	

TODAY'S GOALS:

TODAY'S REFLECTIONS:

TODAY'S AFFIRMATIONS:

Notes

Tuesday

6 am	
7	
8	
9	
10	
11	
12 pm	
1	
2	
3	
4	
5	
6	
7	
8	

Today's Goals:

Today's Reflections:

Today's Affirmations:

Notes

WEDNESDAY

6 am	
7	
8	
9	
10	
11	
12 pm	
1	
2	
3	
4	
5	
6	
7	
8	

TODAY'S GOALS:

TODAY'S REFLECTIONS:

TODAY'S AFFIRMATIONS:

Notes

THURSDAY

6 am	
7	
8	
9	
10	
11	
12 pm	
1	
2	
3	
4	
5	
6	
7	
8	

TODAY'S GOALS:

TODAY'S REFLECTIONS:

TODAY'S AFFIRMATIONS:

Notes

FRIDAY

6 am	
7	
8	
9	
10	
11	
12 pm	
1	
2	
3	
4	
5	
6	
7	
8	

TODAY'S GOALS:

TODAY'S REFLECTIONS:

TODAY'S AFFIRMATIONS:

Notes

SATURDAY

6 am	
7	
8	
9	
10	
11	
12 pm	
1	
2	
3	
4	
5	
6	
7	
8	

TODAY'S GOALS:

TODAY'S REFLECTIONS:

TODAY'S AFFIRMATIONS:

Notes

SUNDAY

6 am	
7	
8	
9	
10	
11	
12 pm	
1	
2	
3	
4	
5	
6	
7	
8	

TODAY'S GOALS:

TODAY'S REFLECTIONS:

TODAY'S AFFIRMATIONS:

Notes

MONDAY

6 am	
7	
8	
9	
10	
11	
12 pm	
1	
2	
3	
4	
5	
6	
7	
8	

TODAY'S GOALS:

TODAY'S REFLECTIONS:

TODAY'S AFFIRMATIONS:

Notes

TUESDAY

6 am	
7	
8	
9	
10	
11	
12 pm	
1	
2	
3	
4	
5	
6	
7	
8	

TODAY'S GOALS:

TODAY'S REFLECTIONS:

TODAY'S AFFIRMATIONS:

Notes

WEDNESDAY

6 am	
7	
8	
9	
10	
11	
12 pm	
1	
2	
3	
4	
5	
6	
7	
8	

TODAY'S GOALS:

TODAY'S REFLECTIONS:

TODAY'S AFFIRMATIONS:

Notes

THURSDAY

6 am	
7	
8	
9	
10	
11	
12 pm	
1	
2	
3	
4	
5	
6	
7	
8	

TODAY'S GOALS:

TODAY'S REFLECTIONS:

TODAY'S AFFIRMATIONS:

Notes

FRIDAY

6 am	
7	
8	
9	
10	
11	
12 pm	
1	
2	
3	
4	
5	
6	
7	
8	

TODAY'S GOALS:

TODAY'S REFLECTIONS:

TODAY'S AFFIRMATIONS:

Notes

SATURDAY

6 am	
7	
8	
9	
10	
11	
12 pm	
1	
2	
3	
4	
5	
6	
7	
8	

TODAY'S GOALS:

TODAY'S REFLECTIONS:

TODAY'S AFFIRMATIONS:

Notes

SUNDAY

6 am	
7	
8	
9	
10	
11	
12 pm	
1	
2	
3	
4	
5	
6	
7	
8	

TODAY'S GOALS:

TODAY'S REFLECTIONS:

TODAY'S AFFIRMATIONS:

Notes

MONDAY

6 am	
7	
8	
9	
10	
11	
12 pm	
1	
2	
3	
4	
5	
6	
7	
8	

TODAY'S GOALS:

TODAY'S REFLECTIONS:

TODAY'S AFFIRMATIONS:

Notes

TUESDAY

6 am	
7	
8	
9	
10	
11	
12 pm	
1	
2	
3	
4	
5	
6	
7	
8	

TODAY'S GOALS:

TODAY'S REFLECTIONS:

TODAY'S AFFIRMATIONS:

Notes

WEDNESDAY

6 am	
7	
8	
9	
10	
11	
12 pm	
1	
2	
3	
4	
5	
6	
7	
8	

TODAY'S GOALS:

TODAY'S REFLECTIONS:

TODAY'S AFFIRMATIONS:

Notes

THURSDAY

6 am	
7	
8	
9	
10	
11	
12 pm	
1	
2	
3	
4	
5	
6	
7	
8	

TODAY'S GOALS:

TODAY'S REFLECTIONS:

TODAY'S AFFIRMATIONS:

Notes

FRIDAY

6 am	
7	
8	
9	
10	
11	
12 pm	
1	
2	
3	
4	
5	
6	
7	
8	

TODAY'S GOALS:

TODAY'S REFLECTIONS:

TODAY'S AFFIRMATIONS:

Notes

SATURDAY

6 am	
7	
8	
9	
10	
11	
12 pm	
1	
2	
3	
4	
5	
6	
7	
8	

TODAY'S GOALS:

TODAY'S REFLECTIONS:

TODAY'S AFFIRMATIONS:

Notes

SUNDAY

6 am	
7	
8	
9	
10	
11	
12 pm	
1	
2	
3	
4	
5	
6	
7	
8	

TODAY'S GOALS:

TODAY'S REFLECTIONS:

TODAY'S AFFIRMATIONS:

Notes

MONDAY

6 am	
7	
8	
9	
10	
11	
12 pm	
1	
2	
3	
4	
5	
6	
7	
8	

TODAY'S GOALS:

TODAY'S REFLECTIONS:

TODAY'S AFFIRMATIONS:

Notes

TUESDAY

6 am	
7	
8	
9	
10	
11	
12 pm	
1	
2	
3	
4	
5	
6	
7	
8	

TODAY'S GOALS:

TODAY'S REFLECTIONS:

TODAY'S AFFIRMATIONS:

Notes

WEDNESDAY

6 am	
7	
8	
9	
10	
11	
12 pm	
1	
2	
3	
4	
5	
6	
7	
8	

TODAY'S GOALS:

TODAY'S REFLECTIONS:

TODAY'S AFFIRMATIONS:

Notes

THURSDAY

6 am	
7	
8	
9	
10	
11	
12 pm	
1	
2	
3	
4	
5	
6	
7	
8	

TODAY'S GOALS:

TODAY'S REFLECTIONS:

TODAY'S AFFIRMATIONS:

Notes

FRIDAY

6 am	
7	
8	
9	
10	
11	
12 pm	
1	
2	
3	
4	
5	
6	
7	
8	

TODAY'S GOALS:

TODAY'S REFLECTIONS:

TODAY'S AFFIRMATIONS:

SATURDAY

6 am	
7	
8	
9	
10	
11	
12 pm	
1	
2	
3	
4	
5	
6	
7	
8	

TODAY'S GOALS:

TODAY'S REFLECTIONS:

TODAY'S AFFIRMATIONS:

Notes

SUNDAY

6 am	
7	
8	
9	
10	
11	
12 pm	
1	
2	
3	
4	
5	
6	
7	
8	

TODAY'S GOALS:

TODAY'S REFLECTIONS:

TODAY'S AFFIRMATIONS:

Notes

MONDAY

6 am	
7	
8	
9	
10	
11	
12 pm	
1	
2	
3	
4	
5	
6	
7	
8	

TODAY'S GOALS:

TODAY'S REFLECTIONS:

TODAY'S AFFIRMATIONS:

Notes

TUESDAY

6 am	
7	
8	
9	
10	
11	
12 pm	
1	
2	
3	
4	
5	
6	
7	
8	

TODAY'S GOALS:

TODAY'S REFLECTIONS:

TODAY'S AFFIRMATIONS:

Notes

WEDNESDAY

6 am	
7	
8	
9	
10	
11	
12 pm	
1	
2	
3	
4	
5	
6	
7	
8	

TODAY'S GOALS:

TODAY'S REFLECTIONS:

TODAY'S AFFIRMATIONS:

Notes

THURSDAY

6 am	
7	
8	
9	
10	
11	
12 pm	
1	
2	
3	
4	
5	
6	
7	
8	

TODAY'S GOALS:

TODAY'S REFLECTIONS:

TODAY'S AFFIRMATIONS:

Notes

FRIDAY

6 am	
7	
8	
9	
10	
11	
12 pm	
1	
2	
3	
4	
5	
6	
7	
8	

TODAY'S GOALS:

TODAY'S REFLECTIONS:

TODAY'S AFFIRMATIONS:

Notes

SATURDAY

6 am	
7	
8	
9	
10	
11	
12 pm	
1	
2	
3	
4	
5	
6	
7	
8	

TODAY'S GOALS:

TODAY'S REFLECTIONS:

TODAY'S AFFIRMATIONS:

Notes

Printed at Repro India Ltd.

Notes